Gary
enjoy
Mark Florida

MW01264267

Christianomics:
Overhaul of the
Economy

MARK FLORIDA

Strategic Book Publishing and Rights Co.

Strategic Book Publishing and Rights Co.
12620 FM 1960, Suite A4-507
Houston, TX 77065
www.sbpra.com

ISBN: 978-1-62212-801-3

Interior Book Design: Judy Maenle

Table of Contents

as pure and faultless is this: to look after orphans and widows in their distress and to keep oneself from being polluted by the world."

With the quickly changing world of international trade and rapid communication, we cannot sustain our greatness by sitting on our laurels. We will have to change the way our government runs things to keep moving forward. There are many significant changes that we can make in the way we manage our economy and the way we take care of our people that will make it feasible to balance our budget and at the same time take care of those in need. The middle class can also be more prosperous and have greater hope for the future.

Areas we need to change radically include the tax system, health care, savings plans, energy and environmental conservation, incentives for our people to excel, and the methods in which we take care of those in need. Innovative ways to reform all of these systems are the theme of this book.

The top of the food chain with respect to managing our money is taxes. The poor should not have to pay any taxes, and the middle class should be able to avoid taxes if they live modestly. That would leave the wealthy and those in the middle class who want to pay taxes left to pay all of the taxes, and they would pay taxes voluntarily if we set up the tax system correctly.

The way to eliminate taxes for the poor would be to eliminate all income tax as well as consumption taxes on the basic needs of life. All taxes should be raised from the consumption of luxuries, "nice to haves," and waste. How to implement this system will be covered in following chapters.

Our health-care infrastructure and technology is great. Our problem is that the cost of health care is unreasonable, and the way it is managed by insurance companies and pharmaceutical companies is appalling. All of our people should have access to the best health care in the world at a cost that is a reasonable percentage of a family's income. There is a way to do this. Some ideas are discussed in future chapters. How would you do it?

Our Social Security system is insufficient to ensure that all of our people have adequate savings for their elder years. I would like to avoid using the "R" word (retirement), as I have retired once so far but am still working. Our system should be set up for future generations so that all of our elderly can live well above the poverty line. The so-called "golden years" are not so golden for many, with the lack of adequate savings and ridiculously expensive care for the elderly, which will bankrupt many who have worked hard all of their lives.

We could replace Social Security with a personal retirement savings account. The account could have a minimum percentage of income invested with a minimum annual yield. Each family's account could be topped up each year by consumption taxes to ensure that income after retirement will keep them above the poverty level.

Some people have a natural incentive to excel in many things. Others need a push. One of the greatest incentives for our economy to grow would be the elimination of income tax. We should tax excessive consumption, not hard work. By taxing excessive consumption, we can provide greater incentive to discourage bad behaviors.

By placing the incentives in the right places, we can also encourage energy and environmental conservation. Taxing waste will provide the natural incentive to reduce waste and provide revenue to replace income taxes. The same principles should apply to businesses that apply to private citizens. This will further stimulate economic growth and employment.

Poverty is unacceptable. There are many people who do not have the opportunity to work or to make a standard of living above the poverty line. This is where generosity comes in to play. Those who have much should give to those who don't. Our laws need to be enhanced through fair taxation to provide for the poor when individual giving is insufficient.

The Lord in heaven is a merciful God. We should also be merciful and help our people live above the poverty level. The Bible says in Romans 12:20–21, "On the contrary: 'If your enemy is hungry, feed him; if he is thirsty, give him something to drink. In doing this, you will heap burning coals on his head.' Do not be overcome by evil, but overcome evil with good." So to pay taxes at the rate corresponding to your tax bracket. There is some merit in discouraging early withdrawal from retirement savings accounts. We want to encourage people to protect their retirement savings; however, there are other ways to do that, such as the personal savings plan that would replace Social Security, which will be discussed later.

The income tax rules as they exist are changing constantly. As an example, many years ago you could deduct interest on credit cards, but that deduction was eliminated after most Americans had run up massive debt on credit cards. It is difficult to keep up with the new tax laws from year to year, and even more difficult to make long-term plans.

One of the few tax deductions left is for the mortgage interest on your home. Most people must have a mortgage in order to "own" a home. However, if you are so lucky as to be able to pay off your house (except for property tax and insurance), then you have to consider if the lack of a mortgage interest deduction will drive you into the next tax bracket. You must do a cash flow analysis to determine if it is better to pay off your mortgage or to pay the outrageous interest so that you can have the tax deduction. Wouldn't it be nice if there were more competition for mortgage interest rates? Ideas for how to provide incentives for interest rate competition are discussed later.

Here is an interesting concept concerning interest rates as described in the Bible in the book of Exodus, chapter 22, verse 25: "If you lend money to one of my people among you who is needy, do not be like a moneylender; charge him no interest."

Income tax rules change with each presidency, and especially when changing from a Republican president to a Democratic president or vice versa. We have rules that will disappear after a certain number of years, mainly timed to coincide with elections. How can you plan your tax strategy when you are not sure which rules will apply in the next few years, let alone the long term? With the elimination of income tax, you won't have to plan your strategies based on changing income tax rules. You would be able to plan your taxes based on how you spend rather than on how you make money. This is a much more positive way to provide incentives for our people to work hard.

A current tax deduction that is good is that for charitable giving. When people help others by charitable giving, they reduce the burden on our tax system to help those in need. After the elimination of income tax, you should get a consumption tax credit for charitable giving, since the amount given should directly result in savings in government aid to the poor.

The Bible says in 2 Corinthians 8:7, "But just as you excel in everything—in faith, in speech, in knowledge, in complete earnestness and in your love for us—see that you also excel in this grace of giving."

All of the schemes that are developed to shelter your money from taxes would be unnecessary if there were no income tax. All kinds of corruption are created by income taxes. Cheating on the preparation of income taxes is an obvious one.

With all taxes moved to consumption, it would be easy to verify that tax receipts are legitimate, since most sales transactions are already managed electronically. You can be sure, though, that there will be a new cottage industry that will develop ways to work around consumption taxes. We will have to figure out how to manage that form of fraud just like any other form of fraud.

It is hard to believe that the US tax system is still better than most other countries. Many of the countries with higher tax rates provide more social programs to their people from their government, so the people in those countries are even worse off because they have less freedom of choice. Do you really want our government to decide how you spend your money? By placing all taxes on consumption, you would have the maximum freedom of choice on how to spend your hard-earned money.

The Bible says in Mark 12:17, "Then Jesus said to them, 'Give to Caesar what is Caesar's and to God what is God's.'" This was based on Caesar's image being on the coin. Well, since the US presidents who have their pictures on our money are dead, I guess we don't need to give it to them.

Paying taxes for Social Security is another form of income tax. I wish I had all of my contributions to Social Security in a savings account yielding 1 percent. But instead I will receive less than the value paid in to Social Security. Then they forget to tell you that if you don't start to withdraw from Social Security by a certain age, you lose money. In fact, you need to figure out for yourself the best year to start withdrawing Social Security to maximize the money that you will receive.

Retirement is a scary thing. If you are fortunate enough to have a savings plan or retirement plan, you must carefully plan your withdrawals so that you won't jump into higher tax brackets. So what if you want to pay off your mortgage after you retire? Well, you will find out that the withdrawal from your retirement accounts would be so heavily taxed if you take the money out all in the same year that you are probably better off paying it off over several years to reduce the tax burden. I did retire once for one weekend. It was short.

People who are unaware of all of the tax laws are vulnerable to excessive and unfair taxation. I am afraid that most people are unaware of even the basic tax laws. There are so many rules that very few people know all of the rules. The system is so complex and many people don't have the resources to minimize their tax exposure.

By converting to consumption tax only, the system will be much simpler and it will be much easier to know what is going on. Most people are highly aware of how much tax they pay when they buy something, especially in the US where the price tag does not include taxes. However, then you are disgusted when you see the actual price including tax. But wouldn't you rather pay all of your taxes based on what you buy?

In many foreign countries, the price listed is the actual total cost including tax. This is nice in a way, but then you have to do a calculation to see how much consumption tax you are paying.

Then there is the inheritance tax or death tax. This is also ridiculous. After you have worked hard to attain wealth and hopefully leave some to your children, then income tax hits again. There should not be any tax at all on money you leave to your loved ones. You have already paid income tax on this money at least once. I would call this tax the second death tax.

An increase in the exclusion for inheritance or "death tax" was introduced by one administration as a so-called benefit, but this is being reduced at the time of this writing. This is one of the so called "tax incentives" that only lasted a few years. You cannot do long-term planning when certain tax laws only exist for only one or two administrations. Administration is a nice term for some of our politicians.

Our government uses income tax rules to "stimulate" the economy. Tax breaks are commonly announced to stimulate the economy while government spending goes up. They try to fool us into believing this is good for our economy in the long run. However, this combination of tax cuts and spending increases only raises our national debt. Why do they do this? It is a short-term ploy to impress some people with the hope of getting re-elected.

Playing with tax cuts and increasing the national debt won't work forever. In fact, now that the US is the largest debtor nation, we are beginning to pay the price for poor fiscal policy. For ideas on how to raise enough money to balance the budget, read on.

The Word of God discusses debt in the book of Romans, chapter 13, verse 8: "Let no debt remain outstanding, except the continuing debt to love one another, for he who loves others has fulfilled the law."

Paying taxes on income just reduces our incentive to work hard and increase our income. We should not be penalized for generating income and contributing to the economy by hard work. People should be encouraged to develop wealth in a straightforward and positive manner. Even the very wealthy should not have to play with the tax system in order to develop their wealth. Shouldn't wealth come directly from hard work and using intelligent business sense?

The elimination of income tax would allow our workers to save the maximum amount of money for food, housing, goods & services, recreation, and retirement. Our people wouldn't be penalized for saving if they didn't have to pay taxes on the interest from savings and the dividends from investments. Our economy would have huge incentives to grow with the elimination of income tax. Competition would flourish much more with the move to consumption tax.

Talk to your congressional representative about getting re-elected based on his or her approach to taxes. One problem with the elimination of income tax is that many people would have to find alternative employment. That is the only problem I could think of. But that would be easy to resolve with incentives created for all kinds of new businesses. Our tax lawyers and accountants could work on how to reduce consumption taxes and developing loopholes for them.

CHAPTER 3

Elimination of Income Tax: Creating Right Incentives

Imagine no tax withholding on your pay stub (or electronic pay advice), and no Social Security tax either.

Without having to worry about income tax, private citizens and businesses would be able to plan how to spend their entire income rather than planning how to spend only the after tax portion. No more withholding from your paycheck for things that you don't need.

So with no income tax, how would our government collect money? That is easy. Taxes could be collected on excessive consumption rather than income. Why do we penalize hard work and good planning with income tax? Instead let's penalize over-consumption of things that are bad for us and excessive luxury. With this plan, the poor could get by without paying any tax. First, income would not be taxed. Second, the consumption of the basic necessities such as food, clothing, shelter, and medical care would also be tax-free.

Middle-class people could also avoid taxes by living frugally. Even the wealthy could avoid tax if they wanted to just store up their money. But don't you think that the rich and famous will continue to spend their money on luxuries? They would be stuck with all of the taxes then. Does that sound fair? Yes!

In the Bible, Jesus told this parable in the book of Luke, chapter 12, verses 16–20: "The ground of a certain rich man yielded an abundant harvest. He thought to himself, 'What shall I do? I have no place to store my crops.' Then he said, 'This is what I'll do. I will tear down my barns and build bigger ones, and there I will store my surplus grain. And I'll say to myself, "You have plenty of good things laid up for many years. Take life easy; eat, drink and be merry."' "But God said to him, 'You fool! This very night your life will be demanded from you. Then who will get what you have prepared for yourself?'"

So what is so Christian about no income tax? Even in Jesus' day they collected taxes. In the Bible, the book of Luke, chapter 5, verses 27–28 reads: "After this, Jesus went out and saw a tax collector by the name of Levi sitting at his tax booth. 'Follow me,' Jesus said to him, and Levi got up, left everything and followed him." In another event concerning Jesus and taxes in the Bible, Matthew 17:24–27 says, "After Jesus and his disciples arrived in Capernaum, the collectors of the two-drachma tax came to Peter and asked, 'Doesn't your teacher pay the temple tax?' 'Yes, he does,' he replied. When Peter came into the house, Jesus was the first to speak. 'What do you think, Simon?' he asked. 'From whom do the kings of the earth collect duty and taxes—from their own sons or from others?' 'From others,' Peter answered. 'Then the sons are exempt,' Jesus said to him. 'But so that we may not offend them, go to the lake and throw out your line. Take the first fish you catch; open its mouth and you will find a four-drachma coin. Take it and give it to them for my tax and yours.'"

Does that sound like a fair way to pay your taxes? This sounds good to me.

The top priority for creating the right incentives to build our economy should always be aimed at our private citizens first. Our people are the foundation of the economy, and their work is the prime driver. The second main driver of our economy is everyone spending their income. People seem to have a natural tendency to spend money, so the best way to stimulate our economy is to allow the people to work and then free up their income to spend it as they wish.

Americans have always been ingenious at finding ways for other people to spend their money. So if we all have more money to spend, there will be more and more ways to spend it. That is ok as long as we take care of our poor at the same time.

The second priority for creating the right incentives for our economy is to stimulate our businesses, which are also made up of people. Businesses need to make a profit to keep going and employ many people. When businesses are profitable, they will naturally grow and continue to employ more people.

With the elimination of income tax, there will be a continuous cycle of growth in the economy. Businesses will be able to plan better how to spend their income, and with additional incentives to employ more people, more jobs will be available. Our workers will have more disposable income to spend on good products (and junk). This will drive more incentives for people to develop better products and further increase competition. This is the way our economy is supposed to work.

Without income tax, savings could be a realistic part of everyone's financial plan. With our current system, most people have to wait and see what is left at the end of the month, if anything, before deciding if they can save any money, even people who have a moderately high income. People who are fortunate enough to have a 401k plan at their place of employment may even be able to supplement their 401k with additional savings if there were no income tax.

Not only should we eliminate income tax, we should also eliminate Social Security tax. Social Security tax could be replaced with a mandatory retirement savings plan. A minimum percentage of our income that people could afford could be invested. The savings account should be set up for the person earning the income rather than using your income to pay for the previous generation.

People could save in this plan up to a much higher percentage of their income than the minimum, based on what they can afford. People who are out of work should have a minimum amount added annually by a consumption tax trust fund. Future generations would pay into their personal retirement plans rather than paying for the people who are currently retired, which is how the Social Security system works now.

Later in the book some ideas are discussed for how to guarantee that the savings plan will have a positive interest rate, even a minimum interest rate. There are ways to hold our financial institutions accountable for fiscal responsibility. These are also discussed in later chapters.

The "Social Security Trust Fund" is a misnomer. It is really just another income tax, and it doesn't matter which of our government's pockets the current Social Security payments come out of.

The required retirement savings plan must have a guaranteed minimum interest rate backed by our government. The plan would have the opportunity to pay out at an interest rate higher than the minimum interest rate. All interest will be tax-free, as it would be considered as income. The annuities paid out to all retirees should be constantly adjusted to keep all of our retirees and elderly above the poverty level.

With the elimination of income tax, including Social Security tax, people will have more disposable income to invest in additional savings plans. Businesses would have the opportunity to provide additional savings packages for employees, as they will not have to worry about Social Security tax contributions and income tax on corporate profits.

The investments in the retirement savings plan must be managed by financial institutions that have the incentive to return the highest reasonable interest rates while being conservative. If losses were to occur in the retirement savings plan fund, our consumption tax trust fund would have to cover the losses. More about how to manage the personal retirement savings plans is discussed later.

A new health-care savings plan system should be set up to cover our health-care costs. This would replace the current Medicare and other insurance systems. Yes, Medicare taxes should also be eliminated, since they are another form of income tax. Medicare would be replaced by each family paying an affordable portion of their own medical costs, and then a health care trust fund would pay the balance of costs out of consumption taxes. For those who are unemployed or retired with minimal income, the health care trust fund should pay all of the costs.

We don't want or need a "national" health care system, which in other countries are inferior to our system, even though we have serious problems with our system. What we do need is an affordable way to pay for our health-care costs.

Americans should be required to pay their own health-care bills up to a reasonable percentage of their income on an annual basis. Beyond that a trust fund should pay the bills. Health-care insurance would no longer be required. With this plan, people will have a cap on how much they will have to pay for medical expenses, and the overall health-care cost to our people will be reduced by eliminating the insurance middleman.

A health-care savings account should be set up for each family or person based on an agreed percentage of income. As with the mandatory retirement savings account, the health-care savings account will be a required deduction from pay. At the end of the year, any unspent portion of each family's health-care savings account would be returned to them to spend or save as they wish.

By having unspent health-care savings returned at the end of the year, our people would have the incentive to seek only needed care. Currently, whatever we pay into health-care insurance is gone, whether you need the care or not. We should also provide incentives for our people to seek preventive care.

The quality of our health care should be the most important aspect of our system. Top quality health care should be available to all of our people. Incentives must be implemented that attract the best talent to the medical and health-care professions. In addition, incentives for medical research must continue and further improve.

With this radical change in how we manage health-care costs, a strong organization must be developed that will manage the quality of health care as well as the costs. This organization should be made up of highly competent doctors and other health-care professionals. The health-care plan will be discussed in more detail in chapter 7.

Another special savings fund should be set up for college education. College savings accounts should also have a guaranteed interest rate and be set up in the same manner as the retirement savings account. College savings funds should continue to maintain early withdrawal rules so that people will be encouraged to keep the funds set aside for education. However, if the funds are determined not to be needed for college, then they could be rolled into one of the other savings plans. The current college savings funds have many flaws, such as negative returns.

The greatest incentive for our people to invest in additional savings plans will be that the interest will all be tax-free.

The elimination of income tax and conversion to consumption tax on luxuries will provide incentives in the right places to encourage people to work hard toward gaining wealth and spending wisely. Then it will be up to each person how to pay his or her taxes.

The necessities of life are described in the Bible in the book of First Timothy, chapter 6, verses 8–10: "But if we have food and clothing, we will be content with that. People who want to get rich fall into temptation and a trap and into many foolish and harmful desires that plunge men into ruin and destruction."

CHAPTER 4

Necessities of Life Tax-free

Our poor people should pay zero tax. Therefore, the basic necessities of life must be free of all taxes. If we replace income tax with consumption tax, then consumption taxes on the basic necessities of life should also be eliminated. It is senseless for the poor to pay taxes and then give some of the money back to them, when in actuality many who need help the most don't get it or what they get is not adequate to live on.

The poor can also be generous. Consider the poor widow in the Bible when Jesus pointed out that she gave more than anyone. Mark 12:43-44: "Calling his disciples to him, Jesus said, 'I tell you the truth, this poor widow has put more into the treasury than all the others. They all gave out of their wealth; but she, out of her poverty, put in everything—all she had to live on.'" And do you think that God would take care of her? I think so.

What are the basic necessities of life? Well, we can discuss and argue about that until the cows come home. However, there are some necessities that are obvious, such as food, clothing, and shelter. And don't forget about health care. There are many other products and services that are good that should have minimal consumption taxes. We should collect the bulk of revenues for our government and trust funds on the consumption of luxuries and products and services that have a negative impact on our society.

With the basic necessities of life being totally tax-free, our people will have more incentive to pursue their basic needs first. All people could theoretically get by without paying any taxes. Most people will still pursue luxuries, "nice to haves," and other

Let our rich people pay the taxes on luxury clothing. The people who must have a hundred pairs of shoes would be stuck with a bit of tax. If you need designer suits, then you can afford to pay the tax.

Shelter

A basic home that is an adequate size for a family should be tax-free, including the elimination of sales tax and property tax. Houses that are larger than necessary for a given family should have a sales tax and property tax. So, those who wish to pay zero tax could buy a basic home tax-free.

If your primary residence is rented, the same rules should apply. Basic housing adequate for the family's size would again be tax-free. If you are renting a luxury home, then you should pay some consumption tax.

Home improvements that are not required should have consumption taxes applied. However, mandatory repairs on a basic home should be tax-free.

Second homes and other real estate investments should have taxes applied onto the purchase. However, capital gains from the sale (income) of any property should be tax-free to the seller. Also, rental income would be tax-free.

If we make basic homes tax-free, we would provide incentives for our contractors to build more affordable homes and would drive more competition into the lower-end market. Those people who can afford to pay taxes could continue to build their dream homes and continue to make profits with their real estate investments.

Listen to what the Lord said to the prophet in the book of Second Samuel, chapter 7, verses 5–7: "Go and tell my servant David, 'This is what the Lord says: Are you the one to build me a house to dwell in? I have not dwelt in a house from the day I brought the Israelites up out of Egypt to this day. I have been moving from place to place with a tent as my dwelling.'"

So the Lord was able to get by without a luxurious house.

Health Care

All necessary health care should be tax-free, including necessary treatments, drugs, home health care supplies, etc. However, elective and cosmetic body work, as well as luxury treatments, should be taxed.

Medicare taxes should be abolished, as mentioned previously. Funding for health care beyond what individuals can afford should be raised through consumption taxes. Chapter 7 discusses ideas for a better health-care plan.

An example of how people can spend all of their money on health care is described in the Bible in the book of Mark, chapter 5, verses 24–29: "So Jesus went with him. A large crowd followed and pressed around him. And a woman was there who had been subject to bleeding for twelve years. She had suffered a great deal under the care of many doctors and had spent all she had, yet instead of getting better she grew worse. When she heard about Jesus, she came up behind him in the crowd and touched his cloak, because she thought, 'If I just touch his clothes, I will be healed.' Immediately her bleeding stopped and she felt in her body that she was freed from her suffering."

Transportation

Transportation is such an important part of our society and economy that basic transportation should be tax-free. This should include the lowest priced car(s) that can accommodate any specific family size. Local mass transit should also be tax-free. We want to encourage mass transit to reduce fuel waste and to encourage people to be more economical.

The purchase of additional cars beyond the number needed for the family should be taxed. Luxury cars with more than the basic needs should also be taxed on purchase. We already have a gas guzzler tax on certain cars, which is a good idea. However, I may never get my mid-life crisis car.

Long distance mass transit travel outside of your home and work area should have some tax, as this could be considered a luxury. Fuels should have a significant sales tax, even more than the current rates. This will encourage people to conserve energy, and it will have a positive benefit for the economy.

With this system, those people who wish to pay zero tax would have the incentive to buy a basic car and use local mass transit for work and shopping. People who can afford to pay for luxury travel will still be able to enjoy their travel. Our government will still raise sufficient funds from luxury transportation.

In many European countries people ride their bikes to work. If people lived closer to work and bicycle lanes were more prevalent, this could be possible in more parts of the USA.

For people and businesses using cars, buses, and trucks for their primary business, then the basic vehicle needs should also be tax-free. Vehicles beyond the basic needs should have consumption taxes applied to the purchase. This will provide incentives for businesses that depend on transportation to thrive when they apply prudent spending on their transportation needs.

Education

High-quality education must be provided for all of our people. Taxes should not be allowed on the pursuit of education. Our government should guarantee excellent education through at least high school, with all needed funding raised from consumption taxes on other goods and services. Wouldn't you rather pay for public schools through consumption taxes than property tax?

Higher education should be encouraged for those who qualify. Students or their parents should not have to pay more than a reasonable percentage of their family income for higher education. We should provide grants to qualified students to cover the costs above a reasonable percentage of family income for higher education.

Scholarships should continue to be encouraged for higher education to defray government and personal family costs. All additional funds required could come from consumption taxes. Wealthy football programs and the like could continue to bring in major funds for universities.

High-quality education is one of the critical foundations of building up our people, which in turn will build the economy. Each person should have access to the highest level of education that he or she is capable of. This will provide the incentive for everyone to achieve to a high level of education without worrying about whether they or their family can afford the best available education.

I am now paying for my fifth child to attend a university. I am hoping that when my grandchildren reach that age, we will have a better system.

The free-market system should continue to be encouraged, and it will be when we eliminate income tax. Moving tax revenues from income to consumption will drive incentives in all sectors of our economy in the right direction to grow and prosper.

CHAPTER 5

Consumption Tax for Luxuries

A better way for our government to raise money is by applying consumption taxes to luxuries, "nice to haves," and products and services that have a negative impact on our society. Other items that are not necessary should also be taxed. Would you rather pay taxes on things you buy or on your income? We definitely should not have to pay taxes on both. The basic needs of life should be completely tax-free.

We could pay taxes for excessive consumption at all levels of government to replace all forms of income tax. Our government would be able to raise as much money as required to balance the budget by applying consumption taxes that correspond to people's spending habits. A balanced budget should be a requirement of our government.

An organization of experts (a person with a briefcase more than 500 miles from home) could be elected (in totally unbiased elections) to recommend which products and services should have consumption taxes. This organization could rank all products and services based on their need, their value to our economy, and whether or not they have an overall positive or negative impact on society.

Some products may have a huge impact on the economy, such as alcohol, but should still have very high consumption taxes because of the negative impact on health (except red wine). I have seen whisky used for medicinal purposes. Have you seen the movie "Three Mules for Sister Sara," where Clint Eastwood uses whisky to numb the pain before the Nun drives the arrow out of him? However, here is a perspective from the

Bible regarding alcohol in the book of Proverbs, chapter 20, verse 1: "Wine is a mocker and beer a brawler; whoever is led astray by them is not wise."

The tax on each product and service could be adjusted regularly so that total government revenues would be sufficient to balance the budget. Balancing the budget is a must.

Items that have negative impact on health, the economy, and the environment should have the highest taxes. These could be followed by items that do not have a negative impact but that add little value or are considered "nice to haves." Then items that have some level of positive benefits to the economy or our general well being, but are not necessary, should have a smaller tax applied.

Items with Negative Impact on Our Health, Environment, and the Economy

Some things that have a negative impact on our health are obvious, such as tobacco. Applying higher taxes on tobacco products would provide added incentive for people to quit smoking. Alcohol is another product that should have high taxes.

Highly processed foods with excessive amounts of sugar and other ingredients that are proven to have a negative impact on health should have high consumption taxes applied. Processed foods that have low nutritional value should have some tax applied. Nutrition experts could help determine the nutritional value of foods for the purpose of setting the consumption tax rates. They should be well paid to attract qualified people and to discourage corruption, but we will always have clever people that can create ways to be corrupt.

Fossil fuels already have significant taxes, however even higher taxes should be set. This would not only raise large sums of money for our government but would also add the incentive for our people to use less fuel. The amount of tax would have to be weighed against the value of fuels to the economy. Since transportation is such a large sector of the American economy, the tax rates would have to be set so that some of our key industries are not put out of business. Reduction of CO^2 (carbon dioxide) and other polluting emissions would be another benefit of fuel usage reduction.

Some consumption taxes would have to be raised gradually over time to allow reasonably slow changes to our economic infrastructure. Many changes introduced through Congress are implemented too quickly without much thought about how the changes will impact everyone. It took us a long time to get our debt to where it is, so it will take time to get us out of debt. However, with the elimination of income tax, the pain of change in consumption taxes would be tolerable.

Alternate energy sources should be encouraged. However, certain ideas such as converting to electric cars will not solve the fuel problem, since we have to burn fossil fuels to produce much of our electricity.

Converting to renewable sources of energy such as wind and solar power should be incentivized with low consumption taxes. Further incentives can be introduced by allowing consumption tax credits for the use of renewable sources of energy.

Luxury items should all have significant consumption taxes on sales. People will not stop buying luxuries, especially if they don't have to pay income taxes. Luxury taxes will add nicely to our government coffers. I always hate it, though, when you are playing Monopoly and you have to pay the luxury tax.

Luxury items add some value to the economy. Some may even provide health benefits, such as recreation and music. Communication and laughter provide emotional benefits as well. A basic cell phone could have a very low tax, but phones with all of the extra gadgets could have a higher consumption tax.

Hear what the Lord did the last time people were communicating freely in the book of Genesis, chapter 11, verses 6–7: "The Lord said, 'If as one people speaking the same language they have begun to do this, then nothing they plan to do will be impossible for them. Come, let us go down and confuse their language so they will not understand each other.'"

Clothing that is luxurious or not necessary, such as accessories, should have significant consumption taxes. Excessive amounts of clothes could also be taxed. Higher-priced clothing could have a graduated tax, and this could encourage the production of lower-priced clothing.

Jesus taught about the value of clothing in the book of Matthew, chapter 5, verse 40: "And if someone wants to sue you and take your tunic, let him have your cloak as well." Again, Jesus talked about worrying about you clothing in the book of Luke, chapter 12, verses 27–29: "Consider how the lilies grow. They do not labor or spin. Yet I tell you, not even Solomon in all his splendor was dressed like one of these. If that is how God clothes the grass of the field, which is here today, and tomorrow is thrown into the fire, how much more will he clothe you, O you of little faith!"

Investment properties not used as a primary residence could have taxes applied on the purchase. However, annual property taxes on investment properties should not be allowed. This will encourage real estate investments. When investment properties are sold, the new buyer would be paying the consumption tax. Taxes on capital gains from real estate investment should not be allowed, as the capital gains are a form of income.

Services should have the same logic applied to determine when taxes should apply. Services that have tangible benefits should have very low taxes, while those considered luxuries should have higher taxes.

An annual review of America's spending patterns could be used to make an annual adjustment to the amount of taxes applied to each product and service. This will ensure that our budget can be balanced.

The IRS would no longer be required in its current form, but it could be replaced by the organization that ranks the products and services for consumption taxes and collects the taxes. An organization would be needed to monitor for fraud in the collection of consumption taxes. This would be an excellent job for many people. With our electronic payment systems, it will be easier to monitor sales transactions and the collection of consumption taxes.

Hear what the Bible says about tax collectors in Matthew 21:31–32: "I tell you the truth, the tax collectors and the prostitutes are entering the kingdom of God ahead of you."

In order to maintain adequate checks and balances, Congress should approve the recommended consumption tax rates at the national level. State and local governments should have limited tax ranges for each product and service that are consistent at all levels of government.

Consumption tax credits should be given for contributions to charitable organizations. These contributions would reduce the burden on our government agencies that help the poor. Private charitable organizations should continue to be encouraged. Other consumption tax credit incentives are discussed in coming chapters.

The replacement of income taxes with consumption taxes is all about allowing people to decide which taxes they will pay. You have heard it said that the only things that you have to do are to die and pay your taxes. Well, I say that you should only have to die (once). In Hebrews 9:27–28, the Bible says, "Just as man is destined to die once, and after that to face judgment, so Christ was sacrificed once to take away the sins of many people."

CHAPTER 6

Personal Savings Plan

The Word of God says in 1 Timothy 5:8, "If anyone does not provide for his relatives, and especially for his immediate family, he has denied the faith and is worse than an unbeliever." Part of taking care of your family is to save wisely. You don't know when you will be out of a job, so you should save consistently and prudently to help out your family if you do lose your job.

Are you happy with the government's savings plan known as Social Security? This is not really a savings plan but another form of income tax. For us to be income tax-free, we will also have to eliminate Social Security taxes. We do need to have savings for all for the retirement years, but there is a better way to do it.

Social Security tax should be replaced with a personal retirement savings plan. A certain percentage of each person's income could be deposited into a retirement savings account. The personal savings plan could be invested such that it actually increases in value over your lifetime, not decrease as it does in the current Social Security system. Your contributions to your personal retirement plan should not be earmarked for paying out to other people who are already retired. Future generations should pay only into their personal savings plan.

We should guarantee a minimum interest rate for funds in the personal retirement savings plan. People could add to this plan up to a much higher percentage of their income based on what they can afford.

People who are out of work could have a minimum amount added annually from the consumption tax fund. The minimum annual contributions to the personal savings plan should ensure that when people reach retirement age, there will be enough in the plan account for them to live on for their retirement years at a standard of living level well above the projected poverty level.

People who have already retired or have worked for many years under the Social Security system should have their retirement savings account topped up so they will have an annuity guaranteed to provide an income for life well above the poverty level. The transition period to convert people to a new personal retirement savings plan from Social Security could be handled quickly with the consumption tax system. People who are currently retired and living solely on Social Security need an immediate boost to give them a decent standard of living.

Funding for topping up everyone's retirement savings accounts should come from the consumption taxes. This would ensure that all of our poor, our retirees, and our disabled people will have a comfortable standard of living for the rest of their lives.

The personal retirement savings account could be supplemented by traditional IRAs, 401k plans, and corporate retirement plans to provide flexibility to workers so that they can manage a large part of their savings plans. People would be encouraged to build wealth, but at least all people could have a minimum reasonable standard of living.

The Word of God says in the book of Proverbs, chapter 13, verse 22, "A good man leaves an inheritance for his children's children, but a sinner's wealth is stored up for the righteous."

With the elimination of income tax, people will have more disposable income to invest in savings plans. Not having to worry about income tax will give our people incentive to spend more wisely (maybe).

You wouldn't have to worry about making an early withdrawal from your 401k or 529 savings plans and paying the penalty taxes, because all savings and interest would be tax-free. In fact, there would be no worry about tax on any of your interest and dividends on savings. Currently, if you make too much money and contribute to a 529 college savings plan, you must pay a tax penalty. That is ludicrous.

The personal retirement savings plan could pay out at an interest rate higher than the minimum guaranteed interest rate if we set it up right. We could develop a competition between investment institutions that would bid on managing portions of the savings funds for, say, five-year stints.

The investment institutions would be required to pay out at least the minimum guaranteed interest rate. If they produce a higher return than the minimum required, they could keep a percentage of the overage. This would provide incentive for the investment firms to make the highest return possible. That way, the investment firm would make a reasonable profit and the owners of the savings accounts would have a good opportunity to make a much higher interest rate than the minimum guaranteed rate. This could be a lucrative way for investment firms to raise capital.

If an investment firm ends up returning less than the minimum guaranteed interest rate over the specified time period, we would revoke their right to manage that portion of the personal retirement savings plan funds. The accounts would be reappointed to other financial institutions that return the highest interest rates. The financial institutions will be required to show fiscal responsibility before being awarded a savings contract, which would be a refreshing change. This will provide additional incentives for investment firms to perform well.

If losses did occur in the overall savings plan fund, we could cover the losses with the consumption taxes.

Additional savings plans could be set up for special needs, such as college funds. These would replace the current 529 plans. The greatest incentive for people to invest in these additional savings plans would be that the interest would be tax-free. Of course, at this writing most 529 plans lose money because you cannot manage them yourself.

College funds may need to maintain withdrawal rules so that they can only be used for education. However, if the beneficiary does not use the funds for higher education by a certain age, then the funds could be rolled into their other retirement savings plans. These additional savings plan funds should be managed in the same manner as the retirement savings plan, with a guaranteed minimum interest payout rate and competition among investment institutions for the right to manage the funds.

It is painful to see how much you have paid into Social Security over your lifetime and then realize how little you get back for retirement. How many people do you know who live comfortably on Social Security alone? The personal retirement savings account with a guaranteed minimum annuity is a better approach to guarantee a comfortable life for all of our elderly and disabled.

Another serious fault of our current system is that people are generally unaware of when they should start withdrawing from Social Security. If you don't start withdrawing by a certain age (62), you will lose part of the benefit. You have to be capable of doing a fairly complex cash flow analysis to ensure that you are not further ripped off by the current Social Security system. This should not be the case, especially for the people who really need it.

The new personal retirement savings account system should start paying out annuities automatically at a certain age, say 60. If people voluntarily retire early, then presumably they have alternate sources of income to carry them over until the payout age. Those people who are laid off at an earlier age should have the benefits start when they are out of work.

Any benefits remaining in the personal retirement savings account when a person dies should be transferred to their beneficiaries. This will provide additional benefits for transfer of estates to your loved ones. Estate taxes should also be eliminated. Wouldn't you rather have your hard-earned money go completely to your loved ones rather than our government?

The Bible tells us that we should be wise managers of our money in Luke 16:1–2: "Jesus told his disciples: 'There was a rich man whose manager was accused of wasting his possessions. So he called him in and asked him, "What is this I hear about you? Give an account of your management, because you cannot be manager any longer."'"

In another Bible passage, Matthew 25:24-27, Jesus teaches a parable about wise money management. "Then the man who had received the one talent came. 'Master,' he said, 'I knew that you are a hard man, harvesting where you have not sown and gathering where you have not scattered seed. So I was afraid and went out and hid your talent in the ground. See, here is what belongs to you.' His master replied, 'You wicked, lazy servant! So you knew that I harvest where I have not sown and gather where I have not scattered seed? Well then, you should have put my money on deposit with the bankers, so that when I returned I would have received it back with interest.'" But Jesus was not just talking about money here, but about serving well, which implies helping others.

Saving for retirement and providing an inheritance for children should be something that can be achieved by all of our people who work hard. Developing a system for people to pay into their own savings plans is a better way to accomplish this. Prudent and accountable management of savings funds is necessary.

CHAPTER 7

Health-Care Plan

Here is Jesus' analysis of being sick in Matthew 9:11-13: "When the Pharisees saw this, they asked his disciples, 'Why does your teacher eat with tax collectors and sinners?' On hearing this, Jesus said, 'It is not the healthy who need a doctor, but the sick. But go and learn what this means: "I desire mercy, not sacrifice." For I have not come to call the righteous, but sinners.'" So is he referring to the tax collectors as being sick?

It is hard to argue that our health-care system is ok. We have great medical technology in America, along with great doctors and health-care professionals. However, the way we pay for medical care is out of control.

The incentives are in the wrong place for managing our health care. Who makes the money in our system? The insurance companies, of course, do very well, but do they add any value to health care? We could add pharmaceutical companies to the list. I recently bought some pharmaceutical mutual funds, and they are the best-performing funds I have.

How about if we eliminate health insurance rather than force everyone to have some? The insurance companies do add some value by negotiating costs of services, but this could be done without insurance. The insurance companies need to make money as long as they are in business, and this only adds to the cost of health care.

Families should pay only a reasonable percentage of their income for needed health care, say up to 10 percent. Beyond that, we could pay the rest of the cost out of a consumption tax health-care fund. However, we don't want a national health-care system like many other countries have. The difference would be that the health-care fund would only pay the bills and not interfere with people getting the best care.

Medicare taxes should be eliminated, since this is another form of income tax. If everyone paid a reasonable portion of their income towards health-care costs, we could greatly simplify the system by eliminating Medicare, Medicaid, and all other forms of health insurance.

All of our people should have access to top quality health-care as needed. We could set up a health-care savings account for each family or person based on a reasonable percentage of income. The health-care savings account could be a required deduction from paychecks. At the end of each year, if you are blessed enough to have an unspent portion of your family's health-care savings account, what would you want to do with it? You would probably not want someone else to keep it, right?

For people who are unemployed or have no income, a health-care trust fund must be set up that pays the total costs. This trust fund would not be like a national health-care system, as many other countries have. This would only be a cash center that pays for our private health-care industry.

Currently whatever money you pay into health-care insurance is gone. If you need to spend more on health care than you paid into insurance for a given year, then you did well. However, if you are healthy and you did not need to spend the amount for health care that you paid into health-care insurance, then you have lost for that year. The main beneficiary of surplus funds is the insurance company.

Health-care insurance does not add any value to the quality of medical care. The insurance companies only collect money and do not provide the right incentives to encourage good medical care. They are out to make money like any other industry, so they only add to the cost of health care.

With the personal health-care savings account and the health-care trust fund, we will have to set up a strong system to ensure fair pricing and an outstanding quality of health care.

A health-care board made up of outstanding doctors and other health-care professionals could be appointed or elected.

The health-care board should be responsible for several important functions. First, they would ensure that people receive the best treatment available. They could provide second opinions if people are unsure if they want or need a recommended treatment. They could also follow up after treatment to look for fraud or unnecessary treatments and prescriptions.

Second, the health-care board should monitor and negotiate reasonable pricing for treatments and prescriptions. However, we don't want pre-approvals to prevent speedy care. People should not have to wait for approvals for treatment. Disputes regarding costs and the need for treatments should be done after the proper care is given. Above all, people should have the right to visit whatever doctor or facility they want to and to seek whatever treatment seems best.

With a board of specialists monitoring the health-care industry, and with the elimination of health-care insurance, the costs should come down over time. The health-care board professionals must be well paid to ensure that we attract top quality people into this organization.

We want our doctors and health-care facilities to make a good income and to provide the best care in the world without taking unfair advantage of the people. We also want to continue to attract the best talent into the health-care professions. Eliminating the costs that have no value will encourage the provision of the best care available.

Qualified young people should receive grants for attending medical schools and other health-care schools. Funding for these grants should also come out of the heath-care trust fund. These grants should continue to be supplemented by private scholarships to encourage the most talented people to enter the health-care professions.

Malpractice insurance for doctors could be significantly reduced. People should be able to file suits for legitimate malpractice cases. However, if doctors had limited liability in such claims, then the good ones could save a tremendous amount of money in reduced liability insurance. The health-care trust fund could make up the difference between the limited liability and any malpractice claims approved by the courts. The health-care board should be involved in the court cases to help determine if claims are valid. True malpractice should still be prosecuted and fined as appropriate.

With limited malpractice liability, competent doctors and other health-care professionals would not have to pay ridiculous premiums to protect themselves, but those who are incompetent or negligent would still need to pay the price. This is another way to reduce the overall cost of health care while at the same time protecting our health-care professionals.

Our medical and health-care research efforts need to continue to be the best in the world. Research projects should receive grants from the health-care trust fund. Private and corporate donations to medical and health-care research should continue to be encouraged. Since there would be no income tax, a good way to provide incentives for private and corporate donations would be to allow consumption tax credits for the donors.

With the personal health-care savings account plan and the health-care trust fund, people will not have to worry about obtaining outstanding health care or about spending their life's savings for a treatment. Our people would have additional incentives to stay healthy and avoid unnecessary care because they will be able to have their unused health-care savings returned at the end of each year.

Additional incentives could be added to the system by allowing the deduction of preventive-care costs from the amount paid out from each family's health-care savings account each year. An even more aggressive positive incentive for our people would be to allow consumption tax credits for preventive care. Preventive care should include exercise programs, nutrition education, routine check-ups, and annual tests as recommended by private health-care professionals and the health-care board.

Long-term assisted health care should be handled in the same way as any other health care. People should only pay a reasonable portion of their income towards long-term assisted health care. To make it simple, long-term assisted health care should just be considered part of the overall health-care plan. The independent health-care board should also monitor the long-term assisted care industry to ensure that costs are reasonable and the quality of care is outstanding.

Our current health-care insurance system is not set up to handle the aging population. The insurance companies will only pay out very limited portions of long-term care costs under normal health-care policies. The cost of buying long-term care health insurance is prohibitive to most people. Even if you think you can afford the supplemental insurance, you are likely to pay in more in your lifetime than you will get back when you need it. After all, the insurance companies need to make a profit also.

Under our current health-care system, if you have insurance, you must pay a significant portion of your income for the insurance in addition to paying Medicare taxes. With most plans, you have to pay deductibles for the health-care services. If you don't have health-care insurance or Medicare, you must have an emergency to be treated.

Another benefit of this plan would be to reduce health-care costs for businesses and corporations. They would no longer have to contribute to health-care insurance for their employees. With the employees' incentives to stay healthier, workers should have fewer sick leaves. This will further stimulate the economy. Businesses and corporations may still want to invest in employees' preventive care to promote a healthier work force and attract the best people. Of course, even healthy people want to have a sick day now and then.

The health-care board could have the incentive to improve the quality of health care and ensure reasonable costs if they were to receive bonuses when there are measured improvements in the health-care industry performance. This would encourage good competition between doctors and health-care facilities.

Wisdom from the Bible on improving health is discussed in the book of Proverbs, chapter 15, verse 30: "A cheerful look brings joy to the heart, and good news gives health to the bones."

This health-care plan would provide excellent checks and balances on the health-care industry while providing the best possible care for all of our people.

If you really have faith, you can follow the Bible's guidelines on healing as described in 1 Timothy 5:23: "Stop drinking only water, and use a little wine because of your stomach and your frequent illnesses."

CHAPTER 8

Corporate Tax Incentives

Can you think of a way to provide incentives for our businesses and corporations to excel and stimulate the economy? What if we also eliminate income taxes for corporations and businesses? If we only impose consumption taxes on the business sector rather than income tax, we will provide huge incentives to get the economy moving.

The same logic used for personal taxes should apply to the business world. The purchase of goods and services that benefit people should have low consumption taxes, while the purchase of goods and services that have negative impacts should have high consumption taxes.

Raw materials and other items that will be used for the manufacture or production of the basic needs, such as natural foods, clothing, shelter, and health-care items should have no consumption tax allowed. With these items tax-free, we will provide incentives for businesses to invest in the development of basic needs. This will greatly reduce their production costs and provide more competition.

Instead of just providing tax breaks for certain pet projects, eliminating corporate income tax and providing the right incentives for the production of the most beneficial products will produce full life-cycle economic benefits.

The purchases of materials and services that are to be used for the manufacture of renewable energy sources such as solar and wind power should have low or no consumption tax. This will help drive down prices for renewable forms of energy, which will in turn drive the growth of those businesses. The purchase of materials intended to be used for the development of public transport should also have low taxes. This will encourage the development of mass transit and further aid in the conservation of energy.

Services provided by people directly should be tax-free. This will drive the incentive to employ more people and less machinery in the service industries. Services that require the purchase of luxury items will already have the consumption taxes built in.

So do you think that with the elimination of income tax for our businesses, the government will have trouble raising enough money to operate? Businesses will still pursue catering to the wealthy with all sorts of luxury items.

Here is what the Bible says about future wealth in Revelation 18:1–3: "After this I saw another angel coming down from heaven. He had great authority, and the earth was illuminated by his splendor. With a mighty voice he shouted: 'Fallen! Fallen is Babylon the Great! She has become a home for demons and a haunt for every evil spirit, a haunt for every unclean and detestable bird. For all the nations have drunk the maddening wine of her adulteries. The kings of the earth committed adultery with her, and the merchants of the earth grew rich from her excessive luxuries.'"

Again, the Bible says in James 5:1–4, "Now listen, you rich people, weep and wail because of the misery that is coming upon you. Your wealth has rotted, and moths have eaten your clothes. Your gold and silver are corroded. Their corrosion will testify against you and eat your flesh like fire. You have hoarded wealth in the last days."

The purchase of materials that are to be used for the manufacture of luxury items should have high consumption taxes. They say that diamonds are a girl's best friend, but they must come with a price. Other areas where we could raise funds in large amounts include the production of tobacco and alcohol.

The purchase of fossil fuels should have a significant consumption tax for businesses and corporations as well as for private citizens. Fuels are a large expense for most industries, and high consumption taxes will encourage conservation and conversion to renewable sources. A significant portion of government funding could come from more taxes on fuel consumption.

Oil and gas production and mineral mining should be taxed at a high rate. This will be a significant source of revenue for our government. However, the profits on the sale of the final products should be tax-free to the manufacturer. The purchase of materials and equipment required for processing and refining of the final products should have a moderate tax. With the elimination of income tax, the sellers of the equipment would not have to pay a tax on their profits. This will give a boost to the processing industries, which typically do not make as much profit as the upstream producers, particularly in oil and gas.

By eliminating income tax for businesses, the incentives will be in the right place for our businesses to succeed. They would be able to avoid high taxes by prudent procurement. With low or no consumption taxes on raw materials for the basic needs, there will be incentives for companies to produce the basic necessities at low prices for the benefit of those who can afford to pay the least. The entire value chain for these items will have lower prices. This will also result in a lower cost for aid to our poor.

With higher consumption taxes throughout the value chain of luxury goods and services, people who can afford the luxury items will be paying the taxes. This will place the tax burden on the wealthy rather than on the poor and the middle class. With the elimination of income tax and implementation of consumption taxes on the development of luxury items, these industries will be able to plan their investments better and allow for more competition.

Company payrolls could be incentivized by providing consumption tax credits for salaries and benefits. This would provide incentives for companies to pay out excellent but reasonable salaries and benefits. The tax credits for employment could be limited to a certain pay level so that lower-paid employees will provide a complete tax credit for their employers. Excessive pay for executives could have the tax credits eliminated. An equitable tax-credit system for payroll would build incentive to hire more low-to-medium salaried employees.

Traditional employee benefits, such as assistance with life insurance premiums and pensions, could also have consumption tax credits allowed. Health-care assistance plans could also be incentivized to supplement the personal health-care savings account. However, luxury benefits for employees should not have consumption tax credits allowed.

Unemployment will be significantly reduced by providing consumption tax credits to employers for hiring people. There will be an economic benefit for companies to hire more people, and this will encourage the use of more people in the work force. Since companies won't be required to pay for health insurance or to supplement Social Security taxes, the overall cost of employment will be further reduced. Companies could still provide other benefits to employees, such as bonuses, savings plans, etc.

The consumption tax credits for employment will improve competition in the marketplace for the best people. With tax credits for employing people and consumption taxes on high-end equipment, the bias can be adjusted so that people will have more economic value to a company than machines to a certain degree. Having more low-and-medium paid employees may be more economical than having a few highly paid people.

The value of our people is described in the book of Matthew, chapter 10, verses 29–31: "Are not two sparrows sold for a penny? Yet not one of them will fall to the ground apart from the will of your Father. And even the very hairs of your head are all numbered. So don't be afraid; you are worth more than many sparrows."

With more people employed, the government burden for social services will be reduced. Hence, the overall consumption taxes could theoretically be lowered over time rather than increased. This should have a full life-cycle effect that gradually employs more and more people, which will reduce the need for government intervention.

Could this be a better way to create jobs than for the president to mandate spending your earnings to create artificial jobs?

Our people must be considered our greatest asset. Companies should be encouraged to invest in our people and view them as being of high value rather than just seeing them as tools or customers. The implementation of the right incentives will lead us in that direction.

Another account in the Bible about the value of people is mentioned in the book of First John, chapter 5, verses 19–20. "We know that we are children of God, and that the whole world is under the control of the evil one. We know also that the Son of God has come and has given us understanding, so that we may know him who is true."

CHAPTER 9

Energy Incentives

By placing significant consumption taxes on fossil fuels, people will have the incentive to conserve fuels. Renewable energy sources must have low or zero consumption taxes. With low consumption taxes on renewable energy sources, people will have the incentive to convert to forms of energy that are better for our world as a whole.

Imported fuels must have significant tariffs above and beyond the consumption taxes placed on domestically produced fuels. This will give an advantage to domestic producers and further discourage the excessive use of fuels.

Hear what the Bible says about fuel in 1 Kings 14:10–11: "I will burn up the house of Jeroboam as one burns dung, until it is all gone."

Energy industries will be incentivized to switch to renewable sources of energy as the demand for these forms of energy rises. With higher demand for renewable sources of energy, the prices will gradually become lower, and eventually the renewable sources will be more economical. Producers of renewable energy sources will have additional incentive by not having to pay income taxes. Further incentives that favor renewable energy sources can be implemented by allowing consumption tax credits on the purchase of goods and services that will be used for the development of renewable sources.

Since fuels are vital to transportation and account for such a large part of our economy, consumption taxes must be increased gradually to allow companies and consumers to switch at a pace that will improve the economy rather than suddenly put millions of our people out of work. Any radical change in the way we manage the economy should be implemented with a gradual process, but not too slow. However, we do need radical changes in our economic system to get us going in the right direction.

Mass transit will need to have the right incentives in place to motivate people, companies, and our government to develop them and to motivate people to use them. The cost of mass transit must be lower than the cost of using your private car to encourage people to switch. Using mass transit can also be fun if well designed.

With no income tax and low consumption taxes on the industries that develop mass transit, the cost and profit incentives will be in place to encourage these systems. With high consumption taxes on fossil fuels, the developers of mass transit will also have the incentives built in to develop the work processes to use renewable sources of energy. If consumption tax credits were allowed for the mass-transit industry, costs for providers and consumers would be even lower.

Convenience must be there for Americans to use mass transit. While a few of our cities have some mass transit, in general the lack of good systems is appalling. In Paris you are never more than 400 meters from a Metro (underground) station. In Oslo you can get anywhere on trains, buses, and trams. London also has a great train, bus, and underground system. In Houston they recently made Interstate10 the widest road (except for the Bonneville Salt Flats) in the world rather than run trains from east to west.

Americans may never give up their muscle cars, but if the right tax incentives are put in place, then those who can afford to pay the taxes will pay the taxes. People who don't want to pay high taxes could use mass transit or convert to more energy-friendly transport.

Converting to electric cars will not be the simple solution. The power companies still need to burn fuel to produce the electricity. Also, the current power grid infrastructure will not support everyone having electric cars.

If a significant percentage of electric power could be generated by solar and wind, then some progress would be made towards energy efficiency. However, generating electricity in large quantities from solar and wind power takes considerable space and favorable weather. New technologies, such as solar-charged batteries and solar-powered production of hydrogen fuel, could also make a positive contribution to renewable energy. Development of new technologies should be incentivized by grants from our consumption tax funds.

All of these ideas will be much better developed by private enterprise rather than being developed by our government. Our government only needs to provide the right incentives for our innovators to come up with the best solutions. A complete restructuring of the tax system with the incentives in the right places would accomplish a major change in the economy and the way we use fuels. Even with the complex and discouraging way we currently pay taxes, our people are still very innovative.

It has taken us many years to develop our infrastructure the way it is. It may take a long time to fix it, so we should start now. With rapid change in the tax structure, it may be very surprising how fast we could improve our infrastructure.

If you want to keep using inefficient cars, you at least would not be paying income tax. Then you would have a choice to lower your overall tax bill with more options for savings.

Wasting of energy should be taxed highly. Flaring of gas and venting of fuels should be measured closely and heavily taxed. Some flaring and venting in industry is required for safety purposes, but if the cost of waste were significant, industries would make the required investments to lower flaring and venting to the minimum possible. Current laws allow minimum flaring and venting, but it would be better to impose high taxes on the waste.

Hydrocarbon vapor recovery systems are common in industry today, but these systems would be even more economical if the tax cost of the waste products was high enough. I have worked in the oil and gas industry for my entire career. In the early days we did not even try to recover the gas in some oil fields because the sales price was so low (pennies per million standard cubic feet). Now that the price of natural gas has nearly equalized with oil, the incentive is there to produce and sell the gas. The artificially low prices of years ago were partly the result of government regulation with the incentives in the wrong places.

There has been some progress in recent years to develop wind farms and solar technologies. However, the US infrastructure in the oil and gas industry is so vast that gasoline has historically been cheaper than bottled water. When you consider the complex processes required to produce gasoline, it is almost unfathomable that bottled water could have been more expensive.

With the right incentives in place, and with the bulk of energy taxes placed on the consumption of fossil fuels, we can greatly reduce the waste of our energy. With higher tariffs on imported fuels and smarter development of our own resources, it is possible to reduce our dependence on foreign oil over a reasonable time period. This will improve the economy in multiple ways: our production of domestic energy will be enhanced, balancing our budget will be easier, and the balance of foreign trade will be improved.

The Word of God encourages the conservation in the book of Proverbs, chapter 21, verse 20: "In the house of the wise are stores of choice food and oil, but a foolish man devours all he has."

CHAPTER 10

Environmental Incentives

Incentives to protect our environment can align with incentives to save energy. If we could set policies that will protect the environment, save energy, and improve the economy at the same time, we would be far ahead. There are ways to do this.

Hear what the Bible says about the original garden in the book of Genesis, chapter 2, verses 8–9; "Now the Lord God had planted a garden in the east, in Eden; and there he put the man he had formed. And the Lord God made all kinds of trees grow out of the ground—trees that were pleasing to the eye and good for food. In the middle of the garden were the tree of life and the tree of the knowledge of good and evil."

And again the Bible says in the book of Revelation, chapter 22, verses 2–3: "On each side of the river stood the tree of life, bearing twelve crops of fruit, yielding its fruit every month. And the leaves of the tree are for the healing of the nations. No longer will there be any curse."

One way to provide incentives to improve and protect our environment is to tax emissions and waste. With the elimination of all income tax, businesses as well as private citizens would be able focus more on projects that will provide improvements to our world, including improvements to the management of our environment.

Placing taxes on emissions and waste disposal would be a much more effective way to improve our environment than implementing regulations that allow certain levels of pollution and waste disposal. The way we operate now, we encourage the implementation of the lowest-cost solution that just barely meets our environmental regulations. The lobby against environmental regulation is tremendous, with special interest groups promoting the watering down of regulations.

With significant taxes on pollution and waste disposal, we would have the incentive to minimize pollution and waste. Meanwhile, the development of alternate work processes that produce less pollution and waste should have very low or zero consumption taxes. It would then be beneficial to invest in lower-polluting and less-wasteful processes rather than just trying to meet a regulatory requirement.

Flaring and venting of natural gas was discussed earlier under energy incentives, and these go hand in hand with environmental incentives. Placing taxes on flaring and venting volumes provides a much better incentive to reduce waste than allowing a certain volume of waste. Processing of permits to develop new facilities would be much faster and more efficient if the result was paying taxes on the waste rather than proving that you will meet the volume regulation with the design.

Emissions of CO_2 (carbon dioxide) are of course the hot topic in the world. Some governments already have CO_2 taxes. This is a definite deterrent to CO_2 emissions. The air emissions of NOX (nitrous oxides) and SOX (sulfur oxides) from major chemical processes are already regulated by limits in volumes allowed. There are many ways to reduce emissions of toxic gases, but the projects are costly. However, if the cost to pollute were to exceed the cost to reduce emissions, then there would be an economic benefit to engage in pollution reduction.

Personal car and truck emissions are another example of significant air pollution. Currently we must pass car emission inspections, which have a positive effect on the environment. However, a better and more positive way to approach the issue is to tax the emissions. People would have the incentive to improve their car performance if it saves them money. With the implementation of higher consumption taxes on fuels, the benefits will be compounded for energy conservation and improvement of the environment.

The discharge of polluting liquids into our water must also be taxed. As with air pollution, if the cost to add pollution-reducing equipment and processes to our wastewater systems were less than the cost to discharge pollutants, then we would pursue the projects that would improve the environment.

We currently allow certain levels of water pollution by regulation. Our incentive with liquid waste discharge is to just barely meet the existing regulations. Listen to what Jesus did with water as described in the Bible in the book of John, chapter 2, verses 7–10: "Jesus said to the servants, 'Fill the jars with water'; so they filled them to the brim. Then he told them, 'Now draw some out and take it to the master of the banquet.' They did so, and the master of the banquet tasted the water that had been turned into wine. He did not realize where it had come from, though the servants who had drawn the water knew. Then he called the bridegroom aside and said, 'Everyone brings out the choice wine first and then the cheaper wine after the guests have had too much to drink; but you have saved the best till now.'"

Now if we could turn pollutants into water that easy, it would be great. But we must have the faith of the size of a mustard seed to do that.

Solid waste is another form of pollution that needs to be addressed. Taxes should be placed on the volume of solid waste disposal and rated according to the toxicity and biodegradability of the waste.

Recycling of solid and liquid waste should be encouraged economically rather than being voluntary. This can be accomplished from two directions. First, taxes on waste disposal volume would encourage recycling. Second, people will want to receive some compensation for usable recycling. There are some good recycling programs in existence, but there is not much incentive economically to reduce waste.

In order to encourage recycling, it must be convenient. For most people this would mean having a service collect the recycled waste from a convenient location. This already exists in some areas, but there is little or no economic benefit to recycle.

Receiving cash back with convenience would encourage people to recycle.

Taxation of pollution and waste is a negative way to encourage the reduction of pollution. A positive way to add to the incentive is to implement no tax or low consumption taxes on pollution reducing projects. Within a given project, consumption of goods and services that provide a positive effect on the environment would have no tax, while the consumption of items that have marginal impact on the environment could have moderate consumption taxes. This would encourage using the most environmentally friendly processes and materials to develop the best projects.

Further incentives could be implemented by allowing consumption and pollution tax credits for pollution reduction projects.

Corrosion and other forms of deterioration of our infrastructure over time should also be discouraged. A positive way to say this is that the prevention of corrosion and deterioration of infrastructure should be encouraged. One of the most obvious forms of corrosion is the rusting of carbon steel. There are many ways to prevent corrosion and deterioration, such as the use of better materials, better coatings, the use of cathodic protection, more frequent preventive maintenance, etc.

In the energy industry, projects typically have a design life of something in the range of twenty-five years. Certain facilities are designed to allow corrosion at a rate that will keep them safe for that design life. For some facilities that may be ok, if there is a plan to remove the facility or upgrade it at the end of the design life. However, critical infrastructure such as buildings, homes, roads, and bridges should have an indefinite design life.

Preventing deterioration of facilities can be encouraged by implementing low consumption taxes on more resistant materials and protection systems. The waste taxes discussed above would also encourage the use of more resistant materials and protection.

Increased taxes on pollution and waste would provide another means of raising money for the government without having income tax. Companies would have the incentive to maximize growth and income and to look at environmental projects as cost beneficial rather than a reduction to the bottom line. Technology improvements and competition would be encouraged by making environmental improvements desirable rather than just something that has to be done to meet the regulations. This would encourage new businesses, which will improve the environment by reducing the costs of the projects. As with any new consumption taxes, the tax rates on pollution must be implemented in a timely manner so that environmental projects are economical but not to the degree that they drive companies out of business. However, it can be expected that certain forms of business that currently thrive on environmentally unfriendly systems will suffer, while many new environmentally friendly businesses will emerge.

How to Avoid Chapter 11: Balancing the Budget

Balancing the budget consists of two major components: responsible spending and adequate funding to cover our spending. I wish it were so easy. In the future, it must be a requirement of our government to have a balanced budget.

Our government must have incentives to balance the budget and to perform well in general. Proposed incentives for our government to perform well will be covered in chapter 12.

Hear what the Bible says about debt in the book of Romans, chapter 13, verse 8: "Let no debt remain outstanding, except the continuing debt to love one another, for he who loves others has fulfilled the law."

Responsible Spending

In order for our consumption taxes to be reasonable, our government must be accountable for responsible spending. Proper checks and balances on government spending are needed.

Our government does need to have the authority to develop the budget and manage spending at a high level, but they should not have absolute power. With the two-party system, there will always be much fighting over the budgets, but the resulting budget is not necessarily the best budget for our country. With our two legislative houses and the president's veto and approval power, there are some checks and balances in place. However, our economy is so complex that it is not likely that Congress and the president are well informed about everything.

One possible solution is to have an independent agency develop the details of the budget, analyze the merits of the spending, and manage the actual spending. Major changes in the budget should require more accountability and should be approved independently.

Our people must have a say in our spending limits. An annual national vote on spending limit increases could be put into place. This would place more accountability on the policy makers to develop reasonable budgets.

What if we would give our leaders incentive bonuses for staying on budget and maintaining responsible spending?

Determining what projects are to be funded is always a difficult process. We have so many ridiculous projects approved that it would be easy to cut spending significantly. Paying reasonable amounts for our projects is also paramount. With an independent agency managing procurement, we could ensure that proper bidding is enforced and reduce corruption when buying goods and services.

No one said it would be easy, but we need to start on a new track soon.

Providing Adequate Funding

The second half of balancing our budget is to produce income equal to or greater than our spending. If we eliminate income tax, all revenue would come from consumption, pollution, and waste taxes.

Annual consumption tax tables could be developed that are based on our consumption statistics in order to provide enough income to ensure that our budget would be balanced. It would be a difficult process to determine fair consumption taxes for the first few years if we convert from income tax. However, the sooner we start, the better. Once we have determined the level of taxes to be placed on the consumption of luxuries, "nice to haves," and waste, it will be easier to adjust the taxes to be fair from year to year.

There will be many factors to consider when developing the consumption tax tables. Some items will be easy to define as luxuries, such as cigarettes and alcohol. Some items will have a desired level of conservation incentives, such as fuels, but fuels are so important to the economy that the taxes must be reasonable to keep various sectors of the economy going.

Consumption tax rates will require annual adjustments as consumer habits change and as prices change. Annual evaluations should result in a bias that will be more favorable to products and services that have a positive impact on our economy and social systems and less favorable to products and services that have more of a negative impact.

By forcing consumption tax totals to match our spending, we can ensure that a balanced budget will be a reality. I don't think we will have a problem with raising the needed consumption taxes to balance the budget. Our wealthy people are still going to buy luxury items, and they will be paying the bulk of our taxes rather than our poor people. What better way to force the taxes on our rich and middle class than to tax our indulgences?

So much for income tax loopholes that allow the wealthy to avoid tax. Oh, the cry of the rich. Our tax lawyers and accountants will not like this system at first. They will have to be employed in other areas. Perhaps they could work for the organizations developing the tax tables for consumption and waste. We will always have fraud to deal with, which will keep many lawyers busy.

The tax collectors could follow Jesus like Matthew did in the following Bible passage in the book of Matthew, chapter 9, verse 10: "While Jesus was having dinner at Matthew's house, many tax collectors and sinners came and ate with him and his disciples."

Balancing the budget for the coming years will not be enough to restore our economy to health. We will also need to eliminate the national debt. This will require taking in more income from consumption taxes than we spend for many years.

In addition, it would be sound for the economy to develop a national surplus.

Many times over recent years there has been a major debate in our government about whether to raise the national debt ceiling or to default. We should never be in this position.

Total forgiveness of our national debt is not going to happen. However, listen to what Jesus said about the forgiveness of debt in the Bible in the book of Luke, chapter 7, verses 41–43: "'Two men owed money to a certain moneylender. One owed him five hundred denarii, and the other fifty. Neither of them had the money to pay him back, so he canceled the debts of both. Now which of them will love him more?' Simon replied, 'I suppose the one who had the bigger debt canceled.' 'You have judged correctly,' Jesus said."

The elimination of our national debt and building of a surplus should be done gradually, but balancing the budget should be required immediately. It has taken us many years to build our national debt, so we should not expect to repair it overnight. However, once we convert from income tax to consumption tax, the elimination of our national debt will accelerate from year to year.

Another example of injustice associated with debt is from the following Bible passage in Matthew 18:25: "Since he was not able to pay, the master ordered that he and his wife and his children and all that he had be sold to repay the debt."

CHAPTER 12

Government Incentives

Can you think of a way to improve the performance of our government? What if we provide our politicians with incentives for good performance? Many of our politicians can stay in office for their entire careers with little accountability for top performance. While many of our leaders do work hard and perform well, others have room for significant improvement to meet the real needs of our country.

Incentives can be positive or negative. Here is a positive incentive as described by God in the Bible in the book of John, chapter 3, verse 16: "For God so loved the world that he gave his one and only Son, that whoever believes in him shall not perish but have eternal life."

Here is a negative incentive from the Bible in the book of Revelation, chapter 16, verses 19–21: "God remembered Babylon the Great and gave her the cup filled with the wine of the fury of his wrath. Every island fled away and the mountains could not be found. From the sky huge hailstones of about a hundred pounds each fell upon men. And they cursed God on account of the plague of hail, because the plague was so terrible."

I suggest that we provide positive incentives for strong performance. The negative incentive is to not vote for those who do a poor job.

With our current political system, our leaders' incentives are misplaced. A key incentive currently is just to get re-elected. Pet projects that may benefit only a few people are all too common. Many projects that we pay for may sound nice, but they add no value to our nation. Many other projects are just ridiculous.

Another quirk of our government is the way riders are added to legislative bills. We never seem to have a new law that is simple and that covers only the real need.

Our lobbying system favors those people who already have money. Lobbying is like advertizing, and the people with the best advertizing usually sell the most.

We should give our politicians incentives to perform well by giving them significant bonuses for positive results. A complete bonus package for our politicians should have several components. Incentives could be implemented in such a way that they are based on improvement of the economy and the quality of life for all.

Corruption in our government could be greatly reduced if positive bonuses were provided for excellent performance.

Following are some factors to consider when providing incentive bonuses.

High Employment Rate

One of the most sought-after goals of our economy should be to place everyone into a meaningful job. One way to increase employment is to provide consumption tax credits for each employee a company hires. With the elimination of income tax, the addition of consumption tax credits, and the reduction in the need for employers to provide health benefits, employers will have the incentive to maximize the hiring of competent people.

If our politicians would receive a significant bonus when the real employment rate goes up, then they would have the incentive to develop the right laws and adjust the tax incentives so that employment does go up from year to year. If the incentives for our businesses are developed properly, jobs will be created naturally through the free-market system rather than having our government trying to create artificial jobs with excessive legislation.

Of course, we would need to have honest reporting of what the real employment rate is. One way our administrations try to look good is by changing the way that unemployment is calculated.

Listen to what the Bible says about how Joseph prospered under the government of Egypt in the book of Genesis, chapter 39, verses 2–6: "The Lord was with Joseph and he prospered, and he lived in the house of his Egyptian master. When his master saw that the Lord was with him and that the Lord gave him success in everything he did, Joseph found favor in his eyes and became his attendant. Potiphar put him in charge of his household, and he entrusted to his care everything he owned. From the time he put him in charge of his household and of all that he owned, the Lord blessed the household of the Egyptian because of Joseph. The blessing of the Lord was on everything Potiphar had, both in the house and in the field. So he left in Joseph's care everything he had; with Joseph in charge, he did not concern himself with anything except the food he ate."

Reduction and Eventual Elimination of Poverty

Having a high employment rate should lead directly to the reduction of poverty. However, in addition to everyone having a job, pay rates must be high enough for each family to be living well above the poverty level. If the employment incentives are invoked and minimum pay rates are implemented so that one worker can keep a family above the poverty level, then most families should be able to avoid living under the poverty level without additional aid from our government.

For our people who cannot work or are not able to work enough hours to stay above the poverty line, government aid could be given so that each family will be above the poverty level. We will always have people who refuse to work. They should receive just enough aid to barely get by.

The definition of poverty needs to be addressed. The basic needs of life should be attainable by all. Having a healthy diet, a high standard of housing and utilities, clothing, health care, and basic transportation should all contribute to the determination of what the poverty level is.

These same critical areas that define the poverty level should also be free of consumption taxes. So the cost of meeting the poverty level will be much lower with the lack of any taxes for these goods and services. With higher demand for tax-free goods and services, companies will have the incentive to produce more of these items, and competition will increase in these sectors of the economy. This will lead to further reductions in prices for the basic necessities.

The guidelines for the poverty level must be adjusted annually so that minimum wages are adjusted and government aid is adjusted to keep up with changes in the economy. A growing economy should stabilize prices, especially with incentives in the right places. The cycle should continue to get better each year for long-term improvement in the economy for all.

Americans are still better off than the rest of the world. With our freedoms, which we have had since the creation of our nation, we have built a strong infrastructure that allows Americans to have abundance and incredible choice. However, that freedom of choice is eroding. We can restore those freedoms with radical changes to the way we manage our government and taxation.

Our politicians should receive significant bonuses for annual improvements in the number of people above the poverty line. Then, when there is no one left below the poverty line, our government should continue to receive bonuses for keeping everyone above the poverty line or for further improvements that keep everyone increasingly above the poverty line.

Reduced Government Spending

Everyone knows that our national debt and increased spending every year is out of control. The amount of wasteful spending is appalling. At present, our government has incentives to approve special-interest projects. Many projects are approved with good intentions, but they should be prioritized in the same manner in which a corporation prioritizes projects. Our corporations are not around long if they don't manage debt and cash flow prudently in order to make a profit. The exception is when our government bails out banks and companies with our money despite incompetence.

Mark Florida

Our politicians must be held accountable to the same financial standards as corporations in order for us to have a healthy economy. Reduced government spending would be easy if the government were held more accountable for spending for each line item.

One place to start is by giving our politicians significant bonuses for reducing spending each year. The bonuses must be determined on the basis that the important projects are funded and that unnecessary projects are not funded. The bottom line of determining the bonuses could be the percentage of reduced spending based on economic growth (GNP).

An independent organization should develop and review the budget and advise which projects are necessary and which are wasteful. This organization should be well paid and consist of economic experts. The usual checks and balances of Congress and the president are also necessary to ensure that funded projects meet the criteria of improving the economy. Congress has too much power in this area. They should produce the laws that protect us but not dictate how the money is spent.

Congress and the president should approve the budget, which is developed and managed by the independent organization. This organization could also determine the level of bonuses that politicians should receive.

Another important aspect of controlling spending is to attain the most value or best prices for necessary projects. A proper bidding process should be applied to all government projects. This should also be overseen by the independent organization to ensure that reasonable bids are received and corruption is eliminated by proper checks and balances.

Our government is supposed to run with checks and balances based on our three branches of government. However, within the legislative branch we need many more checks and balances to reduce spending.

The intention of bonuses will be to reduce spending from year to year. If the economy is running smoothly by the elimination of income tax and proper placement of the other incentives for the private sector to excel, then the need for government spending should naturally be reduced. Inflation would also be kept in check with incentives in the right places to promote competition, reduction of corruption, and by adding more efficiency.

Adjustments in spending for a growing economy would be acceptable, so the government should receive bonuses for reduced spending based on the real value of the economy. This would be an indicator of the health of the economy similar to the financial health of corporations. We need to encourage real economic growth.

Inflation should be discouraged. Increased government spending resulting from price increases on the important necessities should reduce government bonuses. This would give our government the incentive to drive policies that reduce inflation. Inflation on luxuries should be of no concern, as there will be more revenue generated for our government through the consumption taxes on luxuries. Our government should not be spending money on luxuries, so inflation in that sector should not impact government bonuses.

Security is a significant area, and it is difficult to agree on how much is required. Our military budget is incredible. While we all want security, the spending must be controlled. One way to control costs is better management of the spending on what we consider necessary projects. The second is more accountability for what we do with our military. We must focus on inland security and not continue to police the world. Countries that can afford protection and want our protection should pay for our help.

Balanced Budget

A balanced budget is required for a healthy economy. Unfortunately, we are far from that dream. Balancing the budget sounds simple: cash received must equal cash spent. Chapter 11 discusses the balanced budget in more detail.

The previous section discussed reduced spending, which is necessary to bring the spending component to the balanced position. Even with spending under control, cash received will likely have to be increased to balance the budget. That means more tax in the traditional sense. But with the elimination of income tax and replacement of that revenue with consumption taxes, the required revenue to balance the budget can be generated with fairness.

It is interesting that the government uses the method of a tax cut to "stimulate" the economy, even though we can't afford it. However, when a tax cut is made and spending is increased, we are further from a balanced budget. Eventually we will have to pay the price if we don't balance the budget. In fact, we are already paying the price by becoming the biggest debtor nation and having foreigners owning more and more of America.

We can increase government income to balance our spending. By having all taxes raised on the consumption of luxuries and stuff with negative impact, we can set the tax rates required to balance the budget. I would be totally shocked if the wealthy or even the middle-class people reduced their spending on luxuries to an extent that we could not raise the amount of money needed to balance the budget, regardless of what the tax rates were.

I would also be shocked if all people significantly reduced their consumption of alcohol and cigarettes because of high consumption taxes. It would be good if consumption of these items were to be reduced. If our government has trouble raising enough money on the sale of luxuries, then taxes could be raised on the next tier of items that we can call "nice to haves." It would still be better to raise taxes this way rather than taxing income.

Our politicians will have the incentive to balance the budget if they receive a nice bonus. The new financial board managing the budget should also receive bonuses for a balanced budget. This will also give them the incentive to reduce corruption and perform well in defining the budget and the actual spending.

The budget process and bonus system must be reviewed and modified on an annual basis to adjust to rapid changes in the economy.

Interest Rates

Low and consistent interest rates are necessary for a strong and healthy economy. With interest rates changing constantly, it is impossible for individuals as well as corporations and financial institutions to plan their finances. Inflation erodes growth and wipes out investments at conservative interest rates.

Hear what the Bible says about interest in the book of Proverbs, chapter 28, verse 8: "He who increases his wealth by exorbitant interest amasses it for another, who will be kind to the poor."

A key method that our government uses to "check inflation" and "growth" is by controlling interest rates. This has some validity in that out-of-control interest rates would cause all kinds of additional problems. However, placing the right positive incentives into the economy should impact the economy more effectively than playing with the federal interest rates.

With a smooth-running economy, federal interest rates should be constant rather than fluctuating all over the map. Interest rates should not be the main factor used to control the economy. A fair, consistent rate in the range of 3–5 percent should be used for all loans provided by our government. Our government must have the assets to back up money that they loan.

We would not have to borrow money from other countries if consumption taxes were set to balance the budget and foreign trade was equalized. There should not be a requirement for more government bonds in order to keep our government operating. However, if our government wants to provide safe investments, they could provide investment bonds at a strong but conservative interest rate. The capital raised from investors in government bonds must be invested by our government in projects where it will make at least the amount of return so the guaranteed interest rate can be paid back to the investor.

All of our people should be able to borrow from our government at a guaranteed federal rate for necessities such as a primary residence up to a reasonable value. Then all of our citizens could have access to a basic residence with a low interest rate.

Businesses should also be able to borrow from our government at the federal guaranteed rate for high-value projects. However, borrowers of government money must undergo the same scrutiny to ensure they can pay back federal loans as they would have when obtaining loans from private banks.

Private financial institutions and mortgage companies could still provide the bulk of loans. They would have to compete with our government for loans on primary mortgages or other projects approved for government loans. This would encourage competition for loans.

For luxuries or projects that aren't critical, private bankers should be able to charge the interest rate driven by the market. There will be plenty of competition to keep rates low, especially if people can buy a reasonable house at a low guaranteed rate.

Inflation would be controlled better by having consistent interest rates within a certain band. Further control of inflation would be managed by encouraging competition in all of the critical sectors of the economy with the implementation of positive incentives. If people can purchase bonds at a guaranteed payout rate that exceeds the rate they will have to pay for mortgage loans, then investments will increase.

Our politicians could receive bonuses for keeping the interest rates level. A component of the bonus should increase when the number of Americans who invest in government bonds increases. Another component of the bonus could be in effect when the government bond payout rate exceeds the lending interest rate. Still another component of the bonus could be applied when receipts from federal loans are balanced with bond payouts. This scheme would provide incentives for our loan and bond system to be 100 percent internally funded. Having balanced government lending and borrowing along with payout rates higher than loan rates would further stimulate the economy.

As long as our government can invest the bond revenues in private institutions or infrastructure projects that pay out at higher interest rates than the bond rate, the lending rate could become lower over time. If not enough people invest in government bonds to cover the amount paid out in loans, then the balance can be adjusted by consumption tax increases.

Elimination of the National Debt

We must eliminate the national debt. We should not owe anything to other countries, and our government should not owe private citizens more than they have on hand. Having a balanced budget is a key component. Also, having a surplus in foreign trade will be a key factor.

With incentives placed properly to develop our industries, we can reduce and eventually eliminate the national debt. We should not sell our key assets to foreign interests. The starting point of reducing the foreign trade deficit will be to use our natural resources like we used to. We still have large deposits of natural gas and minerals, as well as our incredible farming lands and tourist attractions.

Our greatest resource is our working people. Our education system must be restored and improved so that our great talent will continue to excel. Our people must be recognized as the most important resource that we have. We should be investing heavily in our education system in the same way that corporations invest heavily in advertising. With the employment incentives discussed earlier, another step will be taken to recognize the value of our people.

Our ability to supply food to the world is awesome. Food exports to rich nations should be set at reasonably high prices so that our farmers receive a good income. Domestic prices should remain low as long as our farmers receive a fair price and we favor domestic production rather than imports. However, we should continue to help the poor nations with food aid.

Hear what the Bible says about helping the poor in Luke 12:33–34: "Sell your possessions and give to the poor. Provide purses for yourselves that will not wear out, a treasure in heaven that will not be exhausted, where no thief comes near and no moth destroys. For where your treasure is, there your heart will be also."

Again in the Bible, the wisdom of storing up food during good times is described in the book of Genesis, chapter 41, verses 47–49 and 53–57: "During the seven years of abundance the land produced plentifully. Joseph collected all the food produced in those seven years of abundance in Egypt and stored it in the cities. In each city he put the food grown in the fields surrounding it. Joseph stored up huge quantities of grain, like the sand of the sea; it was so much that he stopped keeping records because it was beyond measure. . . . The seven years of abundance in Egypt came to an end, and the seven years of famine began, just as Joseph had said. There was famine in all the other lands, but in the whole land of Egypt there was food. When all Egypt began to feel the famine, the people cried to Pharaoh for food. Then Pharaoh told all the Egyptians, 'Go to Joseph and do what he tells you.' When the famine had spread over the whole country, Joseph opened the storehouses and sold grain to the Egyptians, for the famine was severe throughout Egypt. And all the countries came to Egypt to buy grain from Joseph, because the famine was severe in all the world."

We should place reasonable import duties at appropriate levels so that foreign businesses cannot dump cheap goods to displace American products. We do not want to eliminate imports; however, our laws should favor American production. With the elimination of income tax and the establishment of low consumption taxes on our greatest resources, production costs will be lower.

Quality standards must be placed on imports as well as domestic products. We should provide consumption tax credits when American manufacturing meets high quality standards. Forcing foreign products to meet high American standards will improve competition. With low prices and high quality, it will be easy to export more than we import.

Balanced foreign trade as well as a balanced budget should be required. We will need to produce a surplus in both areas for some time in order to eliminate the national debt.

Our politicians should receive significant bonuses for reductions in the national debt and eventually the development of a national surplus.

Improved Infrastructure

Our national infrastructure must have proper maintenance to stimulate the economy. America's infrastructure has been crumbling due to the lack of maintenance for many years. We once had the best infrastructure in the world. Now many nations have better maintained infrastructure than America.

Water is the cornerstone of our infrastructure. We should all have quality tap water so that we don't need to buy bottled water. We are not far off from every American having good drinkable tap water. However, the piping infrastructure and treatment plants need to be steadily maintained and new facilities added each year to keep up with growth.

State and local governments should continue to be responsible for top quality local water supplies. When interstate water projects are required, federal assistance should be required. We should start by making the worst areas into the best. Our politicians should receive a significant bonus when there is an increased percentage of Americans who have water meeting high quality standards.

A second key infrastructure needed for good health is proper sanitation. All Americans should have access to good sewage systems and recycling of other waste products. Our government should require efficient public sewage systems in all areas, with improvement projects starting in the worst locations. Local municipalities should be responsible for quality sanitation.

Many rural areas may need septic systems. Consumption tax credits should be made available to people for building and maintaining efficient septic systems.

People need to have incentive to recycle. One way is to tax waste disposal. Another way is to provide consumption tax credits for recycling. Incentives should be provided to our politicians for improved sanitation and reduced waste, starting with the local governments and rolling up to state and federal levels.

Our roads are critical to our transportation network. Driving across the vast USA is a pleasure. Trucking is so important to our economy that we must maintain excellent roads and bridges to keep the transportation industries going strong. The interstate highway system is great as long as it is maintained properly. However, many of our bridges and roads are falling into disrepair.

With the proper implementation of consumption taxes, the funding required for maintenance can be provided. Toll roads should not be allowed. All roads should be free to travel for all of our people and visitors. We can make up the revenue with fuel taxes and other consumption taxes.

Incentives can and should be provided at all levels of government for improvements to our road and bridge infrastructure.

Mass Transit

We have a severe lack of mass transit in the US. To supplement the road system, we should have a quality train system. Incentives need to be provided to encourage the development of rail infrastructure.

A few major US cities have fairly good rail systems, but in some major cities such as Houston, you must have a car to go anywhere. Going from city to city quickly is not feasible without flying.

Many of the European countries have excellent mass transit where you can go anywhere by train, underground, or bus. This includes the countryside as well as the cities.

Our politicians could receive bonuses for improved mass transit. Another component of incentive bonuses could be for the reduced use of fuel.

With the availability of high-quality mass transit, the cost of transportation would come down over time. The use of fossil fuels would also be reduced, and this would feed back into the economy by providing more capital for other projects.

Food

We should all have access to nutritious food. America has incredible farm lands and food-processing infrastructure. The choice of food products in America is amazing. With the elimination of income tax and with no consumption tax on nutritious food, incentives would already be in place to provide low-cost nutritious foods to all of our people.

American farmers should receive a good income to encourage the continuing development of one of our best resources. Fair competition within America and protection from imports being dumped at low prices will help the farmers receive a strong income. Further incentives could be implemented by providing farmers with consumption tax credits for the production of natural foods.

Bonuses should be provided for our politicians when the production and sale of American natural foods increases. This would provide our government with incentives to implement the right laws and favorable tax incentives. Our farmers and consumers will greatly benefit from the right incentives.

Health Care

Medical technology and health-care education in America is second to none. However, affordable health care is another story. Outstanding health care should be a right for all of our people.

Consumption tax credits and grants for medical research should be provided. Medical and other health-care education for qualified Americans should be paid out of consumption tax revenues.

If Americans only had to pay a minimal percentage of their income for health care, then all of our people would have access to excellent care. With free medical education for qualified people, there would be incentive for our most talented people to become health-care professionals. Our health-care professionals should make a good income.

If we can protect doctors from unreasonable malpractice suits, costs could be lowered. If we provided tax credits to doctors who provide outstanding care rather than punishing mistakes, doctors would have the incentive to provide excellent care at reasonable prices.

Bonuses for our politicians could be provided when the percentage of Americans who have excellent health care is increased on an annual basis. This will give our government the incentive to implement the right laws to ensure that quality care at affordable rates is available to all. Bonuses could have a component based on the cost of health care.

Another component of bonuses could be when the average cost of drugs is reduced. The independent health-care board should ensure that drug costs are reasonable. Competition for the production of drugs should be incentivized. When a new drug is developed by a company, they should receive a generous patent fee. Then at least one other company should be given the opportunity to produce the same drug to promote competition.

With a board of professionals auditing the costs and quality of health care, reasonable costs should prevail. With the elimination of health insurance, our money and energy will go into the actual health-care service rather than to the insurance companies.

High Standard of Living, Low Cost of Living

Our standard of living has improved over time for many people, depending on how you define a high standard of living. New technologies and innovation contribute to an improved standard of living. However, the new technologies must be affordable.

New technology is expensive at first, but then the cost comes down when the cost of development is paid out and competition drives down prices. Some good recent examples are computers and flat-screen TVs.

Consumption tax credits can be provided for technology improvements that are shown to have a positive impact on the economy. The free-market system will take care of itself by driving entrepreneurs to develop better products at competitive rates. Innovation should be mostly driven by the free-market system.

Consumption tax credits could be given to companies that sell at lower prices. Then the combination of low sales prices matched with low taxes will drive competitors to find the best pricing to maximize their profit. A component of our politician's bonuses could be for the lowering of the cost of living, especially for the basic necessities.

Superior Parks and Recreation

The national parks of the USA are fantastic. From the Grand Canyon to Yosemite to Rocky Mountain National Park and so on, the USA has the greatest diversity of scenery in the world. We should continue to expand our national parks and national forests, and provide funding for maintenance of the parks. Government bonuses should be provided for the expansion of parks and recreation if they can fund these projects within the balanced budget.

Americans are driven to excel in sports. We have developed the infrastructure and freedom for people to excel in sports. We should keep that edge. Sports stars from around the world come to the USA to train in our universities and other great sports facilities. The competition is fantastic at all levels.

Recreation is another great institution of the USA. In many neighborhoods, there are abundant tennis courts, golf courses, basketball courts, swimming pools, and recreation centers. Most high schools and junior highs have great sports facilities. In Alaska the elementary schools even have ice skating rinks. Most Americans can participate in sports at low cost.

In order to keep our infrastructure strong, we should put in place the incentives. Kids have a natural incentive to excel in sports. Local governments should receive bonuses for improved access to recreation for all of our people.

75

Improved Education

Education is the cornerstone of expanding the economy and building self-esteem among our people. Teachers are our most important resource in education. Incentives for teachers to excel should be provided. Excellent facilities are another motivator for outstanding education. We should provide incentives for developing new schools and improving the quality of all schools, as well as the education systems.

Teachers should be paid as well as industrial professionals. We must provide incentives for our young people to desire to teach. We could provide consumption tax credits for schools when they employ more teachers.

Schools should not have to pay consumption taxes on facilities and programs that will provide positive educational benefits. However, programs and facilities that are deemed to be luxurious or unnecessary could have consumption taxes. The trick is to determine what programs and facilities are positive and which are unnecessary. At least we can agree to disagree.

Incentives for local officials who manage schools could be provided for the administrators of school districts that show excellence and improvement in education. We should start with the worst schools by making them the best. Another component of bonuses should be for the improvement of the quality of the facilities.

With superior education, we will continue to develop energized people, incredible technologies, and a strong economy.

Balance of Trade

Foreign trade will also have to be managed to keep prices in check and improve the economy. Our income from trade should be at least equal to our spending. The free-market system works well when we let it work. Our government can help by placing the right incentives in the right places. America has some distinct advantages. We must focus on those advantages, such as our edge in food supply.

The elimination of income tax will provide a huge impetus to grow our domestic industries. Tax credits will also drive manufacturing in America. Lower prices for American products will result, which will lead us to balanced trade.

An area that is most difficult to manage on a world scale is the cost of oil. Oil is critical to our economy. With such a high percentage of oil imported, we must have more control of the wildly fluctuating prices. With consumption taxes placed on fuels, over time, consumption will even out. We have large reserves of natural gas and a great infrastructure of pipelines. Incentives must be placed so that we continue to develop the resources that we have.

Economic Growth

The elimination of income tax will in itself stimulate the economy. A high employment rate will provide real cash flow to workers who will, in turn, spend more.

Incentives for reasonable pay for all will place more money in consumers' pockets. With less need for government spending, the money flow will be to a larger extent in the hands of our private citizens rather than our government.

Lower interest rates will encourage business investments. Elimination of the national debt and a balanced budget will keep our money at home rather than going overseas, and will encourage spending for excellent projects rather than paying interest on debt.

Valued infrastructure projects will encourage major industrial growth like we had many years ago. A low cost of living will give our people more spending power, and when combined with a better standard of living will encourage even more innovation.

Improved parks and recreation will increase tourism.

With improved education, we will regain our edge in technology development and overall quality of the work force. Improved technology will keep us in the lead with respect to military and security concerns.

Balance of trade incentives along with the balanced budget will improve the economy by keeping our money at home. We will also be sending more goods overseas, which will again stimulate the economy.

Economic growth must be a significant component of bonuses for our politicians.

Management by Independent Organizations

For many of the principles discussed to be put in place and limit corruption, independent organizations must manage the way our government spends money.

Employees of these management boards should be paid as well as professionals in industry and government so they will have the incentive to do their job well and reduce corruption. These employees should receive the same level of bonuses as the politicians who develop the laws that drive an improved economy.

There will always be corruption and new ways invented to be corrupt. We will always have to come up with better ways to stop corruption. This is similar to having antivirus protection on your computer, which must always be upgraded to counter new ways of hacking the systems.

Hear what the Bible says about corruption in the book of Romans, chapter 1, verses 29–32: "They have become filled with every kind of wickedness, evil, greed and depravity. They are full of envy, murder, strife, deceit and malice. They are gossips, slanderers, God-haters, insolent, arrogant and boastful; they invent ways of doing evil; they disobey their parents; they are senseless, faithless, heartless, ruthless. Although they know God's righteous decree that those who do such things deserve death, they not only continue to do these very things but also approve of those who practice them."

Our Assets

Our national assets must be treasured. Our most important asset is our people. By having health, education, prosperity, and the freedom to excel, our people can reach their potential. People must be treated as valuable assets by our government and employers.

Our natural resources are our second great asset. We have incredible resources with our farmlands, minerals, oil and gas, and attractive sites for tourism, water, and recreation. We must use them wisely to conserve them for future generations while stimulating a healthy economy.

Products and services developed by our people are the other great asset. We should be sending more products and services out of the country than we bring in. This will translate into positive cash flow and a healthy economy.

No income tax + positive incentives + education = health + prosperity + the pursuit of happiness.

CHAPTER 13

Aid for Our Poor

With the implementation of a personal retirement savings plan and a responsible health-care plan, everyone should have an income sufficient to stay above the poverty line. Unfortunately, we will always have the poor with us. This is verified in the Bible by Jesus in the book of Matthew, chapter 26, verse 11: "The poor you will always have with you, but you will not always have me."

There will always be many circumstances that contribute to people being in need, even if our basic needs are provided by strong programs. A good way to provide incentives to help the poor will be to allow consumption tax credits for people who donate to our poor people. Contributions to the church and other worthy organizations must have an allowance for consumption tax credits. Such private contributions will reduce the burden on our trust funds.

Besides the basic necessities of life such as food, clothing, shelter, and health care, essentials such as transportation should be available to our poor people. Special public transport for our poor should be encouraged by providing consumption tax credits for the development of the infrastructure needed for these systems. Contributions from the wealthy to provide transport for the poor should also result in consumption tax credits.

We will always have people who fall through the cracks of the best-intentioned programs. Many people are not able to care for themselves. Just providing our poor with money won't solve all of their problems. Many people will spend their money on things that are not good for them, such as alcohol and cigarettes.

There are many good charitable agencies in existence. These should continue to be supported by our trust funds and private donations. Additional assistance should be provided as necessary to ensure that all of our poor people have access to excellent food, clothing, shelter, health care, and transportation.

Hear what the Bible says about helping others in the book of Matthew, chapter 7, verse 12: "So in everything, do to others what you would have them do to you, for this sums up the Law and the Prophets."